D0821682

21st Century
Basic Skills
Library

WE HARVEST PUMPKINS IN FALL

by Rebecca Felix

Cherry Lake Publishing • Ann Arbor, Michigan

1

CHERRY
LAKE
Publishing

Published in the United States of America
by Cherry Lake Publishing
Ann Arbor, Michigan
www.cherrylakepublishing.com

Consultant: Marla Conn, Read-Ability

Photo Credits: AISPIX by Image Source/Shutterstock Images, Cover, Title;
Shutterstock Images, 4, 6, 14; Brandon Bourdages/Shutterstock Images,
8; Natali Glado/Shutterstock Images, 10; Sonya Etchison/Shutterstock
Images, 12; Ken Graff/iStockphoto, 16; Blend Images/Shutterstock
Images, 18; Angelo Marcantonio/iStockphoto, 20

Library of Congress Cataloging-in-Publication Data
Felix, Rebecca, 1984-
  We harvest pumpkins in the fall / Rebecca Felix.
      p. cm. -- (Let's look at fall)
  Includes index.
  ISBN 978-1-61080-906-1 (hardback : alk. paper) -- ISBN 978-1-61080-
931-3 (paperback : alk. paper) -- ISBN 978-1-61080-956-6 (ebook) -- ISBN
978-1-61080-981-8 (hosted ebook)
  1. Pumpkin--Juvenile literature. 2. Pumpkin--Harvesting--Juvenile
literature. 3. Autumn--Juvenile literature. I. Title. II. Series: Felix, Rebecca,
1984- Let's look at fall.

 SB347.F45 2013
 635'.62--dc23

                          2012030459

Cherry Lake Publishing would like to acknowledge
the work of The Partnership for 21st Century Skills.
Please visit www.21stcenturyskills.org for more information.

Printed in the United States of America
Corporate Graphics Inc.
January 2013
CLFA10

TABLE OF CONTENTS

What Do You See?

What fruit do you see?

Fall Season

Fall arrives. Weather gets colder. Many fruits become **ripe**.

Pumpkins Grow

Pumpkins are a fruit. They start as **blossoms**. They grow on **vines**.

All summer, pumpkins grow. They are ready to **harvest** in fall. They are cut from the vine.

What Do You See?

What colors do you see?

10

Color & Size

Pumpkins grow in many colors. Many are orange.

Pumpkins grow to many sizes.
Bree found a big pumpkin!

Kaye goes to a pumpkin patch. She takes pumpkins home.

What Do You See?

What tools are used to make a pie?

Food & Fun

Pumpkin is used in many foods. Jack makes pumpkin pie.

What Do You See?

What shapes do you see?

18

James **carves** pumpkins. He cuts shapes. He puts lights inside.

Winter Arrives

Pumpkins are a fun part of fall. What season comes next?

Find Out More

BOOK

Esbaum, Jill. *Seed, Sprout, Pumpkin, Pie*. Washington, DC:
National Geographic Children's Books, 2009.

WEB SITE

Pumpkins—Enchanted Learning
www.enchantedlearning.com/themes/pumpkin
Find game and activity printouts about pumpkins.

Glossary

blossoms (BLAH-suhms) flowers on a seed plant, such as a
fruit tree

carves (KAHRVS) forms or makes pieces by cutting

harvest (HAHR-vist) to gather crops

ripe (RIPE) full-grown and ready to be eaten

vines (VINES) long stems that wind along the ground or climb

Home and School Connection

Use this list of words from the book to help your child become a better reader. Word games and writing activities can help beginning readers reinforce literacy skills.

arrives	fall	orange	size
big	food	patch	summer
blossoms	fruit	pie	tools
carves	grow	pumpkin	vine
colder	harvest	ripe	weather
color	home	season	winter
cut	lights	shapes	

What Do You See?

What Do You See? is a feature paired with select photos in this book. It encourages young readers to interact with visual images in order to build the ability to integrate content in various media formats.

You can help your child further evaluate photos in this book with additional activities. Look at the images in the book without the What Do You See? feature. Ask your child to describe one detail in each image, such as a color, activity, or setting.

Index

About the Author

Rebecca Felix is an editor and writer from Minnesota. She likes to visit pumpkin patches and pick out pumpkins. Then she carves silly or spooky faces!

24